Camões

Selected Shorter Poems

Shearsman Classics Vol. XXX

Other titles in the *Shearsman Classics* series:

Selected Shorter Poems

of

Luís Vaz de Camões

translated by Jonathan Griffin

with an introduction by Jorge de Sena
& an essay by Hélder Macedo

Shearsman Books

First published in the United Kingdom in 2021 by
Shearsman Books Ltd
PO Box 4239
Swindon
SN3 9FN

Shearsman Books Ltd Registered Office
32 St. James Place, Mangotsfield, Bristol BS16 9JB
(this address not for correspondence)

www.shearsman.com

Shearsman Classics Vol. 30

ISBN 978-1-84861-676-9

The contents of this book first appeared in two
separate publications from The Menard Press:
Camões: Some Poems (1976), ISBN 0 903400 20 0
and *'Gentle Spirit...'* (1980), ISBN 0 903400 56 1
Three previously uncollected translations have been added to
these, with the permission of the Jonathan Griffin Estate,
in addition to the Keith Bosley translation from
Canto 7 of *The Lusiads*.

The new edition has been arranged with the kind permission
of Anthony Rudolf, publisher of The Menard Press.

CONTENTS

Camões: The Lyric Poet

Camões is recognized in Portugal and Brazil as the greatest poet of the Portuguese language. Of course, the greatness of a poet does not depend on how many speak his language today, or ever did; nor does it depend on the specific greatness of the literature written in that language. Nevertheless, even though Brazil was in the first decades of her development when Camões died, and for some centuries Portugal had already had the borders that she maintains today, both countries – not to mention foreign critics and writers – have granted him high and unchallenged rank among the world's great writers. There is something here which, on the whole, people unfamiliar with the Portuguese language and the cultures of Brazil and Portugal do not realise: being the greatest master of that language means to be respected and admired in one of the six or seven most widely-spoken languages in the world today; to be the best writer of a very rich European literature – one of the oldest in Europe – and to be a leading example for literature in Latin America. Maybe, at this point, we could remind readers that Brazil is, in area and population, half of South America and as big as the United States, if one excludes Alaska. The world knows almost nothing about all that, yet it has come to know the name of this poet Camões as being practically the only writer in Portuguese to be mentioned amongst the great 'classics' in any language.

It is quite understandable how this came to happen. While Portugal, isolated between Spain and the sea, tried to become an American, Asian and African power (being the first modern European empire, and the last to crumble, and then only recently), Spain, while developing an American empire, was crucially involved in European affairs. Thus, when newer imperial powers began a campaign of hatred against Spain and Portugal – not, of course, to liberate any peoples, but to take over the spoils – Europe could easily suppress Portugal, while the Spanish had been too much in Flanders, Italy and Germany to be so easily erased. (One hesitates to remind the British that the portrait of Philip II of Spain hangs rightfully among the portraits of the kings of England, one of whom he was for a time.)[1] If Camões could survive that process and remain known, it was because he had written a very complex epic poem, *The Lusiads,* which is still one of the great, and indeed even readable, epics of modern times, even if its complexity has baffled many readers throughout the ages. But very rarely was the world aware that this epic poet deserved also the highest rank for his lyric poetry, not to mention the interest, for the history of European theatre, of the three plays attributed to him.

The body of his lyric poetry (if we include only what is undoubtedly his) amounts to a total of some 14,000 lines,[2] against the nearly 9,000 lines of the epic poem. This represents an enormous output, a sea of writing from which one can truly say that many towering masterpieces emerge. Even in the lighter or more occasional compositions, when the permanent undercurrent of sadness and despair that is so much Camões' own does not come through, the writing never fails to demonstrate an extraordinary level of elegance, wit, and gracefulness. It is strange that such a well-travelled man – although he was no more than a common soldier – who lived in the East for nearly twenty years, and certainly could not carry with him a humanist's library, wrote so much, and almost always at such a level of cultural refinement. If we count the epic poem, the lyric poetry, and just the verse parts of his plays, we must come to the conclusion that this adventurer was a compulsive writer. During some 30 years of active life (from, say, his early twenties until the last years of his life in Lisbon, which we may suppose to have been quite barren, due to disease and distress), he wrote an average of 800 lines per year, under the

---

[1] Philip was, for four years, co-monarch of England and Ireland with Queen Mary, but was only king by *jure uxoris.* His regnal rights lapsed on the death of Mary. Sena is right however that English history tends to obscure the co-monarchy, which sits awkwardly in the popular narrative of post-Henrician history. *[Editor]*

[2] c. 200 sonnets, 10 Petrarchan *canzoni,* 8 large eclogues, a dozen odes, seven or eight elegies in *terza rima,* four compositions in *ottava rima,* one sestina, more than a hundred short lyrical poems.

most adverse conditions. An adventurer, yes, but also – if one may paraphrase Patrice de la Tour du Pin[3] – a man who is a 'recluse in his poetry'. And whether in his epic poem or in his lyric pieces, this is exactly what he is – the obsessive *persona* that he created in his own writings.

What we really know about him is minimal, and almost anything beyond what we describe below is nothing but a 'soap-opera' devised by delirious biographers. He was a poor member of a noble family, well connected with the grandees of Portugal and Spain. The family's origins date back to a Galician noble who took refuge in Portugal at the end of the 14th century, who is supposed to have been one of the important poets of that period – although his works are now lost. The place and date of Camões' birth are uncertain, undocumented; the accepted view is Lisbon, around 1524–25. We know that he died in Lisbon in 1580, or perhaps in 1579. Nothing is known of any formal studies – most annoying for critics who are always searching for the *alma mater* of great writers (who in general have had a special knack for avoiding academic trappings) – in spite of the richness and profundity of his culture, so much a part of his creations. In his youth he served in the Portuguese possessions in North Africa, where he lost an eye in a skirmish with the Moors. He left for the East in 1553. At that time he was under arrest for taking part in a street brawl in which a royal officer had been assaulted. The King's pardon – one of the few relevant documents that have come down to us – describes the incident succinctly, and declares that the offender is willing to go to India, in the King's service. None of his wanderings for almost 17 years in the East – 'India' meant everything from the east coast of Africa to the Far East – is documented; we have only hints, and second-hand information. In 1569, the great historian Diogo do Couto, who never mentioned him elsewhere in his accounts of military deeds by the Portuguese in the East, states that he found him stranded in Mozambique, and helped to pay for his journey back to Lisbon, where he must have arrived in 1570, with the epic poem which he was to publish in 1572.

[3] Patrice de la Tour du Pin (1911–1975) was a prominent French writer and poet.

On account of his service in India, and not merely to reward him for *The Lusiads*, as is commonly said, the King – by now the legendary Sebastian to whom the poem is dedicated – granted him a royal pension. His mother, long a widow and who outlived him, had the pension renewed in her name. He never married, nor did he father any known children. All of his works – other than *The Lusiads* and presentation poems written to introduce books by two of his friends, one being curiously enough a great work of science published in Goa, 1563, and the other the first printed Portuguese treatise on Brazil (Lisbon, 1576) – were left unpublished at his death. Two plays were printed in 1587. But the bulk of his lyric and less than lyric poems collected at random in several manuscripts – no autograph is known – only began to appear in 1595. This process continued for three centuries, with nearly every writer in Spain and Portugal in the 16th and 17th centuries being ransacked to enrich Camões' supposed output, until a critical outcry put an end to it. This started a revision of authorship which is still incomplete – and, because of the confusion or lack of attributions in the known manuscripts, it may, in many cases, never be complete. The doubts, however, leave unscathed almost all of the most beautiful, important, or memorable poems.

If we know very little of Camões, biographically speaking, we know everything of his poetic *persona*, as few poets at any time have transformed themselves, their experiences and their thoughts, into such a revealing work of art as Camões' poetry is. A great mistake of the critics of the past, in their frustration at the lack of documentation on his life, was to look into his poetry for the missing information. Certainly, here and there he mentions some particular circumstances – with, of course, no date attached – but that is integrated into the creation of a self which speaks far more about feelings, ideas, judgements of life, stressing in the Renaissance and Mannerist fashion personal experience at a very abstract and intellectual level, although charged with tremendous emotion. The emphasis on that experience in Camões attains a force rare among poets anywhere in the 16th century, but is in tune with the main trends of Portuguese literature at the time

– of which his work is the culmination. This is understandable because, from the beginning of the 15th century, the Portuguese – with their involvement in the discoveries and conquests that they had started for Europe – had developed a sense of 'reality' at variance with the learned tradition, owing to their contacts with new lands and peoples and, as a great Portuguese cosmographer of the time said, 'new stars'. The ideological and aesthetic foundation of Camões' poetics lies in a fusion of personal experience, Platonic philosophy, esoteric and Pythagorean views of the universe, an extensive and well-digested array of classical allusions and myths, an extremely personal and spiritualised Christianity – but not a dogmatic Catholicism – and Petrarchan modes of form and expression. Camões also uses the traditional Iberian form of *redondilha*,[4] not confining himself to the Italian models which he took to superlative and individualised perfection. What is especially striking is the fact that we can speak of 'harmony', since this poetry – where it is not just graceful play – voices a terrible anguish and despair, a sense of the world being out of joint, and a deep conviction of personal and inescapable fate, of the poet and the man as a paradigm of human suffering and frustration; in Camões' work these typical Mannerist contradictions reach a most impressive and moving level of expression. Camões' language commands all linguistic levels from the most colloquial and direct to the stately resounding stanzas of *The Lusiads*, passing through the painful utterances of the major lyric poems. He is never too sweet, nor he is too convoluted in his diction, even if, in this last respect, playing with concepts is one of the devices that he sometimes uses to convey deeper insights into the mind at work, the heart feeling, the poet hearing himself. That language

---

[4] The seven-syllable line (eight in Spanish, as Portuguese metrics does not count the last unstressed syllable) is used by Camões for his lighter and shorter pieces, with an extraordinary exception: his paraphrase of the psalm *Super flumina Babylonis,* a long composition in which the rendering of the psalm is transformed into a most personal poem, at the same time an evaluation of his life as a man and a poet, and an exposition of his philosophical ideas on salvation, which stands as one of the most beautiful masterpieces in the Portuguese language.

is so precise and flexible, that it is said any poet in Portuguese, if and when he attains a superior command of poetic expression, may look like an imitator of Camões here and there, even though Camões may not have influenced him at all.

For a long time – his finest 17th century critics knew better – Camões' lyric poetry has been considered as no more than fine 'love poems', and indeed many of his poems do deal with love at different levels. (Some of the more sexually explicit passages in *The Lusiads,* and in certain minor pieces, have always shocked the prudish.) And, since Camões poses constantly as the lover in distress, disdained by his lady, separated from her by the great spaces of earth and time, it was quite easy – at the price of forgetting many major poems or entire passages from others – to understand those poems in the 'romantic' way: the unhappy man, unrecognised by society, persecuted by fate and by unfulfilment in love; or to view many of them as clever exercises in the Petrarchan tradition. The greatness of Camões lies in being all that and much more – with the proviso, of course, that Romanticism had not been discovered in his time. Camões is, in the most existential way, a philosophical poet, deeply concerned with finding a meaning for a world that seemed, at the sunset of the Renaissance, more and more meaningless – a meaning that he achieves *structurally,* imposing the order and equilibrium of his poems on the disorder of that world. He is also deeply concerned with the very workings of the human mind, to the understanding of which he brings a startlingly modern approach to Platonic dialectics, one which looks like a divination of Hegel. He is concerned, above all, with ultimate values in this world, and (eventually) in the next – which he views as an abode of peace, purity and love. So erotic, so sexually obsessed, so pagan, and so free in moral judgements about 'sin', Camões is in fact a moralist, for whom Christianity (a very peculiar blend of Jewish kabbalistic leanings, neo-Platonism and Christology) is above all charity, tolerance, and forgiveness. For him, a 'saint' is anyone, of any religion or race, who is faithful to his own character, has a sense of mission, and is willing to sacrifice himself for the good of others and for his own beliefs – but can also be a nymph who surrenders herself to sexual embraces... So, the poet of love in Camões is the singer, and many times more poignant at that, the singer of the ultimate love: love as knowledge, love as something more widely embracing than God himself. No doubt he courted many ladies, and enjoyed the favours of many who were less than ladies, as is quite transparent in many of his poems (and unashamedly mentioned in his correspondence), but love, for him, is something that transcends everything – life and literature, experience and religion, Platonism, Christianity, Petrarchism – to become the very essence of human life and of the universe, with all the pangs and frustrations, all the yearnings and joys.

This is the poet whom the narrow visions of Portuguese nationalism and Catholicism, taken for granted by many foreign critics, have been unable to detect in the magnificent structure of *The Lusiads*, in which pagan gods are *real*, being the visual representations of the attributes of the unattainable God. This too is the poet who, lamenting unrequited love, or weeping for a dead lover, was really feeling the tragic identity between ultimate love and nothingness. Behind the modes and fashions of his time, which, as we have already said, he made so personal – being at the same time much more concerned with expression than with mere displays of artistry, notwithstanding the tremendous pride in his own genius that can be detected in many utterances – this is Camões' great *persona*, much greater than the very greatness that has been recognised as his. Whether that *persona* is the real man matters very little. No great poet is more real than his own poetry, when what he writes touches the deeper chords of human existence, either in its happier and most carefree moments, or in the utter darkness of absolute despair and loneliness. And then, when nothing remains but dreams and memories that are no longer of any help, only the writing of poetry may remain – and this is precisely the theme of one of the most splendid and moving, and the longest, among his Petrarchan songs.

To translate Camões is an extremely difficult task. One may be tempted to assimilate him to some of his contemporaries in other languages, who shared much of his culture and his stylistic approaches, and in the process lose the personal transfiguration

15

imposed by Camões on everything that he absorbed or imitated. Or one may be a little baffled by his shifts in mood, his ironic playfulness, the rigorous logic of his musings along with sudden jumps that may seem carelessness. And this last 'or' may lead one to miss one of the main characteristics of Portuguese poetry, of which he is the highest culmination. Since the earliest times – represented in the medieval song-books that are one of Europe's greatest treasures – Portuguese poets, at their best, were never concerned with art for art's sake, but always with poetry for poetry's sake. Craftsmanship – and Camões ranks among the best craftsmen in any literature – was never, for the greatest among them, anything more than what was needed for poetry to be written, experience of life to be conveyed, and the poet to become more of a man than himself. If brilliance comes into that, and many times it did, it is only because the upsurge of poetry required it. Jonathan Griffin, a most distinguished poet himself, a sensitive and experienced translator, and also a man concerned with moral issues and the place of man in this world, has, I believe, avoided all those possible mistakes in his translations, since he knows Portuguese poetry so well. And, in giving a modern English voice to the lyric Camões, as he has done here, he has made of him exactly what Camões knew that he was and wanted to be: a poet of any time and any place.

In one of his most famous lines, Camões said that he had left his life scattered throughout the world. To add a last stroke of irony to that, destiny played even with his bones. His modest tomb in one of Lisbon's churches vanished in the terrible earth-quake of 1755. When, in preparation for the celebrations of the third centennial of his death, in 1880, his Portuguese admirers looked for his remains, everything was uncertain. And, to celebrate the great event, the bones transferred with pomp and circumstance to a lavish tomb placed in the Jerónimos monastery – a splendid building erected in Lisbon at the beginning of the 16th century, near the beach from which Vasco da Gama, the hero of *The Lusiads*, left for his glorious voyage to India – those bones are certainly not those of Camões. So what happened with his remains is what had happened with his life: his lyric poetry left scattered and unpublished when he died, and, one might say, his poetic personality left in the hands of many biographers and critics. Now – and paradoxically the celebrations of the fourth centennial of *The Lusiads* in 1972 have helped – Camões is rising from the dead like a phoenix. Let us hope that this selection of his poems will start his resurrection as a great lyric poet for English readers. Much in his epic poem has aged for our time, but nevertheless, it still remains an extraordinary achievement whose fascinating secrets – very different from the 'official' interpretations – are still a long way from being unravelled. But nothing has aged in his lyric poems, other than superficial modes and turns of style and there, as in many passages of the epic poem, we have a man speaking to us, a complex human being at that, in the way that only great poets do, about anguishes, hopes and despairs that are very much akin to our own today.

JORGE DE SENA
Santa Barbara, California,
November 1975

Em quanto quis Fortuna que tivesse

Em quanto quis Fortuna que tivesse
Esperança de algum contentamento,
O gosto de hum suave pensamento
Me fez que seus effeitos escrevesse.

Porém temendo Amor que aviso désse
Minha escriptura a algum juizo isento,
Escureceo-me o engenho co'o tormento,
Para que seus enganos não dissesse.

Ó vós, que Amor obriga a ser sujeitos
A diversas vontades! quando lerdes
N'hum breve livro casos tão diversos;

(Verdades puras são, e não defeitos)
Entendei que segundo o amor tiverdes,
Tereis o entendimento de meus versos.

As long as Fortune wishes

As long as Fortune wishes that I may
possess in me hope of some delectation,
the savouring of a sweet cogitation
makes me write its effects; I write away.

Yet Love, fearing what I write could convey
to any shrewd judgement a hint of caution,
darkens with torment my imagination,
that those deceits of his I may not say.

O you whom Love obliges to be subjects
to various wills! If and when you read, told
in one short book, occurrences so various,

they are pure truths, they are, and not defects...
Know, too according to the love you hold is
the understanding you'll have of my verse.

Redondilha

Pus meus olhos numa funda,
E fiz um tiro com ela
Às grades de uma janela.

Uma dama, de malvada,
Tomou seus olhos na mão
E tirou-me uma pedrada
Com eles no coração.

Armei minha funda então,
E pus os meus olhos nela;
Trape! Quebrei-lhe a janela.

Redondilha

Put my eyes in a sling
I did, and let fly with it
At the bars of a window.

Certain lady, just to hurt me,
Took her eyes in her hand,
And a stoning she has shot me
With them to my heart.

Then this sling of mine I manned
And I put my own eyes in it,
Crash, I have smashed her window.

Redondilha

Catarina bem promete;
Eramá! como ela mente!

Catarina é mais fermosa
Pera mim que a luz do dia;
Mas mais fermosa seria,
Se não fosse mentirosa.
Hoje a vejo piedosa;
Amanhã tão diferente,
Que sempre cuido que mente.

Catarina me mentiu
Muitas vezes, sem ter lei,
E todas lhe perdoei
Por uma só que cumpriu.
Se como me consentiu
Falar-lhe, o mais me consente,
Nunca mais direi que mente.

Má, mentirosa, malvada,
Dizei: para que mentis?
Prometeis, e não cumpris?
Pois sem cumprir, tudo é nada.
Nem sois bem aconselhada;
Que quem promete, se mente,
O que perde não no sente.

Jurou-me aquela cadela
De vir, pela alma que tinha;
Enganou-me; tinha a minha,
Deu-lhe pouco de perdê-la.

Redondilha

Caterina promises,
damn it! what a liar she's!

Caterina's lovelier
than the light of day to me;
how much lovelier she'd be
if she just were not a liar.
Today I see she's mercy's flower,
tomorrow so different – I
always think she tells a lie.

To me Caterina has lied
many times, owning no law,
yet I've forgiven her them all
for only one when she kept word.
If, as to me she has allowed
speech, what should follow she allows,
never more will I say she lies.

'Cruel girl, liar, vile,
Why is it you lie?' I said,
'Promise, and not keep your word?
Not fulfilled, nothing's worth while.
You're not very well-advised;
She who promises and lies is
not aware of what she loses.'

That I *shall* come at that bitch
I have sworn by the soul I had,
I gulled myself, for mine she has –
gives not a damn about losing it.

A vida gasto após ela.
Porque ma dá, se promete;
Mas tira-ma, quando mente.

Tudo vos consentiria
Quanto quisésseis fazer,
Se esse vosso prometer
Fosse por me ter um dia.
Todo então me desfaria
Convosco; e vós, de contente,
Zombaríeis de quem mente.

Prometeu-me ontem de vir,
Nunca mais apareceu;
Creio que não prometeu
Se não só por me mentir.
Faz-me, enfim, chorar e rir:
Rio quando me promete,
Mas choro quando me mente.

Mas pois folgais de mentir,
Prometendo de me ver,
Eu vos deixo o prometer,
Deixai-me vós o cumprir:
Haveis então de sentir
Quanto a minha vida sente
O servir a quem lhe mente.

After her my life I pitch –
she gives it to me with each promise,
but when she lies she takes it from me.

'All things I would let you do,
Whatever you might have a mind to,
If for once your promise meant you
'd not ... keep *from* me, some day,
 with you, then, I would undo
myself, all, and have you, well pleased,
jeering at anyone who lies.'

Promised me yesterday to be
together – since then no glimpse of her,
I think she's made no promise ever
if not just to lie to me.
Makes me cry and laugh to see;
laugh I do when she promises,
but I cry when a lie it is.

'But since you do like to deceive
(vowing you'll see me with such art),
I leave you the promise part –
the fulfilling you'd best leave
to me: and then you will perceive
how much more there is to please
one who keeps word than one who lies.'

Transforma-se o amador na cousa amada

Transforma-se o amador na cousa amada,
Por virtude do muito imaginar:
Não tenho logo mais que desejar,
Pois em mim tenho a parte desejada.

Se nella está minha alma transformada,
Que mais deseja o corpo de alcançar?
Em si somente póde descansar,
Pois com elle tal alma está liada.

Mas esta linda e pura semidea,
Que como o accidente em seu sojeito,
Assi com a alma minha se confórma,

Está no pensamento como idea;
E o vivo e puro amor de que sou feito,
Como a materia simples busca a fórma.

The lover's self-transformed

The lover's self-transformed to the thing loved
By virtue of imagining on and on.
So I have nothing more to crave to obtain,
Since here in me the craved portion I have.

If into that my own soul finds itself
Transformed, what more's the body hoping to gain?
Since with it it has such a soul bound in,
In its own company it can rest relieved.

And yet this ravishing pure demigoddess
Who, like the accident being displayed
In its subject, with my soul does conform,

Remains in my philosophy like Ideas,
And this living and pure love I am made of
Like simple matter searches for the form.

Está o lascivo e doce passarinho

Está o lascivo e doce passarinho
Com o biquinho as pennas ordenando;
O verso sem medida, alegre e brando,
Despedindo no rustico raminho.

O cruel caçador, que do caminho
Se vem callado e manso desviando,
Com prompta vista a setta endireitando,
Lhe dá no Estygio Lago eterno ninho.

Desta arte o coração, que livre andava,
(Postoque ja de longe destinado)
Onde menos temia, foi ferido.

Porque o frecheiro cego me esperava,
Para que me tomasse descuidado,
Em vossos claros olhos escondido.

There, ordering his feathers

There, ordering his feathers with his beak,
Perches the wanton gentle little bird,
Calmly and cheerfully, quite without dread,
Lavishing from the rural spray his lyric.

The cruel hunter, from the beaten track
Turning aside, steals up, docile, unheard,
Sights quick the arrow, and on him has bestowed
Eternal nesting in the Stygian lake.

By that same skill this heart, when moving free
(Although already from afar marked out),
Has been pierced, where it least felt any fear;

For the blind archer stayed waiting for me
(That he might catch me negligent of doubt),
Hidden within your eyes which are so clear.

Aquella triste e leda madrugada

Aquella triste e leda madrugada,
Cheia toda de mágoa e de piedade,
Em quanto houver no mundo saudade
Quero que seja sempre celebrada.

Ella só, quando amena e marchetada
Sahia, dando á terra claridade,
Vio apartar-se de huma outra vontade,
Que nunca poderá ver-se apartada;

Ella só vio as lágrimas em fio,
Que de huns e de outros olhos derivadas,
Juntando-se, formárão largo rio;

Ella ouvio as palavras magoadas,
Que puderão tornar o fogo frio,
E dar descanço ás almas condemnadas.

That sorrowful and cheerful break of day

That sorrowful and cheerful break of day,
Simply with heartbreak and with mercy filled
As long as there be yearning in the world
I would have her be solemnised always.

She alone, when-gentle, sparkling, gay –
She emerged bringing brightness to the world,
Saw split away one will from the other will
That never may see itself split away.

She alone saw the tears, which in a thread
Springing from one and the other pair of eyes
Augmented to a great broad river

She saw the words heartbreak itself said,
Which had been able to make fire freeze
And bring to the condemned souls a reprieve.

Cançao VII

Manda-me Amor que cante docemente
O qu'elle ja em minh'alma tem impresso
Com pressuposto de desabafar-me;
E porque com meu mal seja contente,
Diz que ser de tão lindos olhos preso,
Contá-lo bastaria a contentar-me.
Este excelente modo de enganar-me
Tomara eu só de Amor por interesse,
Se não se arrependesse
Co a pena o engenho escurecendo.
Porém a mais me atrevo,
Em virtude do gesto de qu'escrevo;
E se é mais o que canto que o qu'entendo,
Invoco o lindo aspeito,
Que pode mais que Amor em meu defeito.

Sem conhecer Amor viver soía,
Seu arco e seus enganos desprezando,
Quando vivendo deles me mantinha.
O Amor enganoso, que fingia
Mil vontades alheias enganando,
Me fazia zombar de quem o tinha.
No Touro entrava Phebo, e Progne vinha;
O corno de Acheloo Flora entornava;
Quando o Amor soltava
Os fios d'ouro, as tranças encrespadas,
Ao doce vento esquivas;
Os olhos rutilando chammas vivas;
E as rosas entre a nove semeadas;
Co'o riso tão galante,
Que hum peito desfizera de diamante.

Canzone VII

Love commands me to sing about with sweetness
What, lately, in this soul of mine He imprinted,
His expectation being to ungrieve me;
And, to have me reconciled with my sickness,
Says, since I am by such fair eyes imprisoned,
To sing of this would by itself relieve me.
This excellent contrivance to deceive me
I would, direct from Love, gladly have taken,
Except that He might darken
My genius with pain's pen, having changed His stand.
And yet I venture out,
In virtue of that signal I write about.
And if I sing more than I understand,
I invoke the fair looking
That has more power than Love has in my lacking.

I was used to live without recognising
Love, making light of his bow and his cheats
When living by them was what kept me alive.
I played the part of a fraud love, surprising
A thousand others' wills by such deceits –
I laughed at anyone caught by this love.
Phoebus was entering Taurus, Procne arriving,
Flora wreathing the horn of Achelöus;
It was then Love let loose
The gold threads – at the sweet wind the curled tresses
Playing at hard-to-get;
The eyes – it's living flames they radiate;
And, sown in places among snow, the roses;
With such a gallant laugh –
A breast of diamond it would dissolve.

Hum não sei quê suave respirando,
Causava hum admiravel, novo espanto,
Que as cousas insensiveis o sentião.
Alli as garrulas aves, levantando
Vozes não ordinarios em seu canto,
Como eu no meu desejo, s'encendião.
As fontes crystallinas não corrião,
D'inflammadas na vista linda e pura;
Florecia a verdura
Que andando co'os divinos pés tocava;
Os ramos se baixavão,
Ou d'inveja das hervas que pizavão,
Ou porque tudo ant'ella se baixava.
Não houve cousa, emfim,
Que não pasmasse della, e eu de mim.

Porque, quando vi dar entendimento
Ás cousas que o não tinhão, o temor
Me fez cuidar qu'effeito em mi faria.
Conheci-me não ter conhecimento;
Porém só nisto o tive, porque Amor
Mo deixou para ver o que podia.
Tanta vingança Amor de mi queria,
Que mudava a humana natureza
Nos montes, e a dureza
Delles, em mi por trôco traspassava.
O que gentil partido,
Trocar o ser do monte sem sentido,
Por o que'm juizo humano estava!
Olhae que doce engano!
Tirar commum proveito de meu dano.

Assi qu'indo perdendo o sentimento
A parte racional, m'entristecia
Vê-la a hum appetite submettida.

A what was it? I don't know, smoothly breathing,
Was causing a strange, a new marvelling
Which even the insensitive things were feeling.
Where I was, the garrulous birds, raising
A turbulence of voices, in their singing
Became, as I in my desire, flames flying.
The crystalline fountains were now not flowing
But turned to still fire at the fair pure sight.
With blooms the green grew bright
Where the divine feet touched it in her wending.
Downwards the branches bowed –
Either in envy of grasses those feet trod,
Or because before her all things were bending.
Not a thing, finally,
But was amazed at her, and I at me.

For when I saw understanding being given
To things which had none, awe made me ask myself
What alteration in me there might be.
I knew myself not to have knowledge; even
So I had some – so far only as Love
Allowed it me, that His power I might see.
Love was requiring such revenge from me
That here He was, making human nature change to
Mountains, while in exchange
Their hardness into me, over, He heaved.
O what a gentle dealing,
To exchange a mountain's being-without-feeling
For what in a human judgement lived and moved!
Trick far from merciless,
To draw general profit from my loss!

So that, with feeling losing gradually
Hold of the rational part, I grew sad
Seeing that part to an appetite surrendered.

Mas dentro n'alma o fim do pensamento,
Por tão sublime causa, me dizia
Qu'era razão ser a razão vencida.
Assi que quando a via ser perdida,
A mesma perdição a restaurava:
E em mansa paz estava
Cada hum com seu contrário em hum sogeito.
Oh gráo concêrto este!
Quem será que não julgue por celeste
A causa donde vem tamanho effeito,
Que faz n'hum coração
Que venha o appetite a ser razão?

Aqui senti d'Amor a mor fineza,
Como foi ver sentir o insensivel,
E o ver a mi de mi proprio perder-me:
E, emfim, senti negar-se a natureza;
Por onde cri que tudo era possivel
Aos lindos olhos seus, senão querer-me.
Despois que ja senti desfallecer-me,
Em lugar do sentido que perdia,
Não sei que m'escrevia
Dentro n'alma co'as letras da memoria,
O mais deste processo,
Co'o claro gesto juntamente impresso,
Que foi a causa de tão longa historia.
Se bem a declarei,
Eu não a escrevo, d'alma a trasladei.

Canção, se quem te ler
Não crer dos olhos lindos o que dizes,
Por o que a si s'esconde,
Os sentidos humanos (lhe responde)
Não podem dos divinos ser juizes,
Senão hum pensamento
Que a falta suppra a fé do entendimento.

But in my soul the end of thought, really
For so sublime a cause, patiently said
That it was reason Reason should be routed.
So that, just when the way was being rated
Lost, by that perdition it was restored:
And there in mild peace rested
Each along with its contrary in one subject.
O! here's great harmony!
Will ever anyone not judge heavenly
A cause whence comes alteration so huge, it
Can, in a heart, occasion
Appetite to arrive at being reason?

Lo, here I felt the 'live finesse of Love,
What it was like to see insensibles feel;
And see myself become my own self-loser;
In the end I felt Nature unsay itself:
Which made me believe all was possible
To her fair eyes, except choose me to serve her.
I felt myself fainting away, and after –
'stead of the feeling I was forfeiting –
Something unknown was writing
In my soul, in the characters of memory,
The main part of this process
With the clear signal there imprinted closest,
Which has been cause for such a lengthy story.
I, if well I've described it,
Am not its writer, from the soul transcribed it.

Song, should your reader not,
Of the fair eyes, believe what you announce
Through what in him lies hid,
Human perceptions (you must answer him)
Cannot be judges of the divine ones,
Unless with one thought starting:
Faith overcomes failure in understanding.

O ceo, a terra, o vento socegado

O ceo, a terra, o vento socegado,
As ondas que se estendem por a areia,
Os peixes que no mar o sono enfreia,
O nocturno silencio repousado;

O Pescador Aónio que, deitado
Onde co'o vento a água se meneia,
Chorando, o nome amado em vão nomeia,
Que não póde ser mais que nomeado,

Ondas, (dizia) *antes que Amor me mate,*
Tornae-me a minha Nympha, que tão cedo
Me fizestes á morte estar sujeita.

Ninguém responde; o mar de longe bate;
Move-se brandamente o arvoredo;
Leva-lhe o vento a voz, qu'ao vento deita.

The sky, the land, the wind

The sky, the land, the wind soothed down…
The waves along the shore stretching away…
The fishes, curbed by sleep in the sea's sway…
The silence, settled to rest, of day done…

The Fisherman Aónio who, lain
Where the wind and the water play the old game,
Sobbing, names in vain the beloved name
Which now can be no more than named alone:

Waves, he kept saying, *before Love kills me*
Restore to me my Nymph, whom you so soon
Took from me and lo be death's subject chose.

No-one answers him. Far and wide the sea
Beats. Timber is gently stirring. The wind
Snatches his voice, which on the wind he throws.

Alma minha gentil, que te partiste

Alma minha gentil, que te partiste
Tão cedo desta vida descontente,
Repousa lá no Ceo eternamente,
E viva eu cá na terra sempre triste.

Se lá no assento Ethéreo, onde subiste,
Memoria desta vida se consente,
Não te esqueças de aquelle amor ardente,
Que ja nos olhos meus tão puro viste.

E se vires que póde merecer-te
Alguma cousa a dor que me ficou
Da mágoa, sem remedio, de perder-te;

Roga a Deos, que teus annos encurtou,
Que tão cedo de cá me leve a ver-te,
Quão cedo de meus olhos te levou.

Gentle spirit, my own

Gentle spirit, my own, who went and parted
So quickly from this life, unfulfilled so,
There in Heaven eternally repose
While I live here on earth always sad-hearted.

If memory of this life be permitted
There in the ethereal seat to which you rose,
Do not forget the burning love whose glow
So pure, in these eyes of mine, you once sighted.

And if some consolation ever seem to
You deserved by the grief flooding me through,
The hopeless heartbreak of you missing to me,

Implore God, Who has made your years so few,
As quickly to take me from here to see you
As He did quickly from my eyes take you.

Que poderei do mundo ja querer

Que poderei do mundo ja querer,
Pois no mesmo em que puz tamanho amor,
Não vi senão desgôsto e desfavor,
E morte, em fim; que mais não pode ser?

Pois me não farta a vida de viver,
Pois ja sei que não mata grande dor,
Se houver cousa que mágoa dê maior,
Eu a verei; que tudo posso ver.

A Morte, a meu pezar, me assegurou
De quanto mal me vinha: ja perdi
O que a perder o medo me ensinou.

Na vida desamor somente vi,
Na morte a grande dor que me ficou:
Parece que para isto só nasci.

What can I now ask

What can I now ask from the world for me,
Since just there where I placed enormous love
All I've seen's disappointment and dislove,
Then death itself; for no more can there be?

Since, with living, life does not surfeit me,
Since I now know that great grief does not kill,
If there's a thing can give greater grief still
See it I shall, for all things I can see.

Death, despite me, assured me of the full
Evil that was coming to me; already
What taught me to lose fear I've lost and miss.*

In life I've seen nothing except dislove
In death the great grief which for me was steady
It seems that I was only born for this.

Or: What losing fear taught me I've lost and miss.

Sextina

Foge-me pouco a pouco a curta vida
Se por caso he verdade qu'inda vivo;
Vai-se-me o breve tempo d'ante os olhos;
Chóro por o passado; e em quanto fallo,
Se me passaõ os dias passo a passo,
Vai-se-me, enfim, a idade, e fica a pena.

Que maneira tão aspera de pena!
Pois nunca hum'hora vio tão longa vida
Em que do mal mover se visse hum passo.
Que mais me monta ser morto que vivo?
Para que chóro, emfim? para que fallo,
Se lograr-me não pude de meus olhos?

Oh formosos, gentís e claros olhos,
Cuja ausencia me move a tanta pena,
Quanta se não comprende em quanto fallo!
Se no fim de tão longa e curta vida
De vós m'inflammasse inda o raio vivo,
Por bem teria todo o mal que passo.

Mas bem sei que primeiro o extremo passo
Me ha de vir a cerrar os tristes olhos,
Que Amor me mostre aquelles por quem vivo.
Testimunhas serão a tinta e penna,
Qu'escrevêrão de tão molesta vida
O menos que passei, e o mais que fallo.

Oh que não sei qu'escrevo, nem que fallo!
Pois se d'hum pensamento em noutro passo,
Vejo tão triste genero de vida,
Que se lhe não valerem tanto os olhos,

44

Sestina

Fleeting it is, bit by bit, my short life,
If by chance it is true I am still living.
Brief time's escaping me before my eyes;
I mourn for what is past, and while I speak
The days are passing by me, pace by pace.
My span's escaping, what stays is the pain.

What a curious, sour sort of pain!
For never an hour saw so long a life
Taken by a man to move from ill one pace.
Would I be any better dead than living?
Why do I mourn, in fact? Why do I speak
If I've failed to beguile me with my eyes?

O! beautiful, gentle and limpid eyes
Whose absence drives me on to such a pain –
It measures how great only when I speak!
If, at the end of so long and short life,
I were, ev'n then, inflamed by your ray, living,
I'd judge good all the ill through which I pace.

But well I know that first the final pace
Must come to me and close these my sad eyes,
Before Love shows me the eyes for whom I'm living.
They will be witnesses to ink and pain
Which will write down, from a backbreaking life,
The least I passed through and the most I speak.

O! I don't know what I write or what speak!
For if from one to another thought I pace
I keep seeing so sad a kind of life
That, could it not count on such strength of eyes,

Não posso imaginar qual seja a penna
Qu' esta pena traslade com que vivo.

N'alma tenho contino hum fogo vivo,
Que se não respirasse no que fallo,
Estaría ja feita cinza a pena;
Mas sôbre a maior dor que soffro e passo,
O temperão com lágrimas os olhos:
Com que, se foge, não se acaba a vida.

Morrendo estou na vida,
          e em morte vivo;
Vejo sem olhos,
          e sem lingua fallo;
E juntamente passo
          gloria e pena.

I can't imagine what would be the pen
That would transcribe the pain in which I'm living.

In my soul always I've a fire, living,
And, if this did not breathe in what I speak,
Ash would be all that's now left of the pain.
But over the worst grief I endure and pace
There bend, tempering it with tears, the eyes,
By which, though fleeting, not ended is life.

Dying I am in life,
                        and in death living,
I see without eyes,
                        and without tongue speak;
And at the same time pace through
                        glory and pain.

Erros meus, má Fortuna, Amor ardente

Erros meus, má Fortuna, Amor ardente
Em minha perdição se conjurárão:
Os erros e a Fortuna sobejárão;
Que para mi bastava Amor somente.

Tudo passei; mas tenho tão presente
A grande dor das cousas, que passárão,
Que ja as frequencias suas me ensinárão
A desejos deixar de ser contente.

Errei todo o discurso de meus anos;
Dei causa a que a Fortuna castigasse
As minhas mal fundadas esperanças.

De Amor não vi senão breves enganos.
Oh quem tanto pudesse, que fartasse
Este meu duro Genio de vinganças!

My errors, bad fortune, fiery love

My errors, bad fortune, fiery love
Together have conspired to my destruction;
There was no need of errors or of fortune,
Love alone would for me have been enough.

I've passed through all, but retain so alive
The great pain of the things which did pass on,
Their haunting furies have taught me this lesson,
Not to want to be happy again ever

I have erred the whole discourse of my years;
I've given Fortune cause to castigate
My expectations founded on my eagerness.

Of love I have seen nothing but brief lures,
Might someone have the power to satiate
This my implacable vindication genius!

O cysne quando sente ser chegada

O cysne quando sente ser chegada
A hora que põe termo á sua vida,
Harmonia maior, com voz sentida,
Levanta por a praia inhabitada.

Deseja lograr vida prolongada,
E della está chorando a despedida:
Com grande saudade da partida,
Celebra o triste fim desta jornada.

Assi, Senhora minha, quando eu via
O triste fim que davão meus amores,
Estando posto ja no extremo fio;

Com mais suave accento de harmonia
Descantei por os vossos desfavores
La vuestra falsa fe, y el amor mio.

When the Swan

When the Swan feels he has arrived before
The hour that sets limit to his living,
A larger harmony, a voice wholly grieving
He lifts up for the uninhabited shore.

He longs to cheat and of life enjoy more
And, mourning the farewell of this life, feeling
In him the great melancholy of leaving,
Celebrates the sad ending of this journey.

So, my Lady, when I began to see
The sad ending, all my loving has granted,
And me already at the ultimate twine,

With sweetest ever stress of harmony
For your disfavours I descanted
Shame on *your false faith and this love of mine.*

Correm turbas as águas deste rio

Correm turbas as águas deste rio,
Que as rapidas enchentes enturbárão;
Os florecidos campos se secárão;
Intratavel se fez o valle e frio.

Passou, como o verão, o ardente estio;
Humas cousas por outras se trocárão:
Os fementidos fados ja deixárão
Do mundo o regimento, ou desvario.

Ja o tempo a ordem sua têe sabida;
O mundo não; mas anda tão confuso,
Que parece que delle Deus se esquece.

Casos, opiniões, natura, e uso,
Fazem que nos pareça desta vida
Que não ha nella mais do que parece.

The waters of this stream

The waters of this stream are running clouded,
By those of the heavens and those of the high hills stirred up;
The meadows that were thick with crops have dried up;
Intractable the valley has grown, and cold.

Spring has gone, gone the Summer whose heat scalded;
Some things with other things have suffered swap;
Always perfidious, the Fates have let slip
The government or lunacy of the world.

Time has its own order, known in advance;
The world not-but goes on confused as if
God forgets it, it has dropped from His aims.

Nature and custom, opinions and chances
Make it seem to us, as regards this life,
That in it there is no more than what seems.

Em prisões baixas fui hum tempo atado

Em prisões baixas fui hum tempo atado;
Vergonhoso castigo de meus erros:
Inda agora arrojando levo os ferros,
Que a morte, a meu pesar, tëe ja quebrado.

Sacrifiquei a vida a meu cuidado,
Que Amor não quer cordeiros nem bezerros;
Vi mágoas, vi miserias, vi desterros:
Parece-me que estava assi ordenado.

Contentei-me com pouco, conhecendo
Que era o contentamento vergonhoso,
Só por ver que cousa era viver ledo.

Mas minha Estrella, que eu ja agora entendo,
A Morte cega, e o Caso duvidoso
Me fizerão de gostos haver medo.

I have done time

I have done time in more than one vile prison,
Fettered – shameful correction of my errors,
Even now, dragging behind me, I carry
Irons which death has, to my sorrow, riven.

I have sacrificed life to my obsession,
For Love is not content with lambs or heifers;
Seen heartbreaks, seen hardships, fresh exiles ever
Seem to have been ordained to this profession.

I have contented me with little, knowing
Of course contentment was a shameful thing,
Just to see what cheerful living was like.

And yet my Star, to me how plainly showing,
Blind Death, and Accident the bewildering,
Have made me a man who flinches from delights.

Na ribeira do Euphrates assentado

Na ribeira do Euphrates assentado,
Discorrendo me achei pela memoria
Aquelle breve bem, aquella gloria,
Que em ti, doce Sião, tinha passado.

Da causa de meus males perguntado
Me foi: Como não cantas a historia
De teu passado bem, e da victoria
Que sempre de teu mal has alcançado?

Não sabes, que a quem canta se lhe esquece
O mal, indaque grave e rigoroso?
Canta, pois, e não chores dessa sorte.

Respondi com suspiros: Quando crece
A muita saudade, o piedoso
Remedio he não cantar, senão a morte.

By the waters of the Euphrates

By the waters of the Euphrates on and on
I sat and was discoursing through my memory
Still the same brief good, always the same glory
Which formerly I passed in you, sweet Sion,

I was being questioned about the reason
Of my ills: – Why are you not singing the story
Of your past good, and of the victory
Which then, over your ills, you always won?

Don't you know, one who sings is soon without
His ill, though it be heavy, rigorous?
Sing, then, – weeping for that is waste of breath.

With sighs I answer: – When the copious
Regret goes on growing, the one devout
Remedy is … not to sing if not death.

Cá nesta Babilónia donde mana

Cá nesta Babilónia donde mana
Matéria a quanto mal o mundo cria;
Cá donde o puro Amor não têe valia;
Que a Mãe, que manda mais, tudo profana;

Cá donde o mal se affina, o bem se dana,
E póde mais que a honra a tyrannia;
Cá donde a errada e cega Monarchia
Cuida que hum nome vão a Deos engana;

Cá neste labyrintho onde a Nobreza,
O Valor e o Saber pedindo vão
Ás portas da Cobiça e da Vileza;

Cá neste escuro caos de confusão
Cumprindo o curso estou da natureza.
Vê se me esquecerei de ti, Sião!

Here in this Babylon

Here in this Babylon, from which there flows
Matter for every ill the world creates,
Here where as 'not of value' pure Love rates
Since all things the supreme Mother defiles;

Here, where good's self-damned, in tune evil is,
And more than honour tyranny has its way;
Here, where Monarchy, blind and astray,
Thinks by a void name it clears itself;

Here in this labyrinth, in which nobility
And knowledge and endeavour, each, goes fawn
At the doors of turpitude and cupidity;

Here in this shadowy chaos of confusion,
I keep the course of nature and fulfil it.
See if I ever shall forget you, Zion!

O dia em que nasci moura e pereça

O dia em que nasci moura e pereça,
Não o queira jamais o tempo dar;
Não torne mais ao Mundo, e, se tornar,
Eclipse nesse passo o Sol padeça.

A luz lhe falte, O Sol se [lhe] escureça,
Mostre o Mundo sinais de se acabar,
Nasçam-lhe monstros, sangue chova o ar,
A mãe ao próprio filho não conheça.

As pessoas pasmadas, de ignorantes,
As lágrimas no rosto, a cor perdida,
Cuidem que o mundo já se destruiu.

Ó gente temerosa, não te espantes,
Que este dia deitou ao Mundo a vida
Mais desgraçada que jamais se viu!

May the day I was born die

May the day I was born die and be done,
Never find room in time again, once dead,
Not return to the world, if return it should,
Let eclipse, at that tread, smother the Sun.

Let light cheat it, on it the Sun turn dun,
The world show signs of sinking to conclude,
Monsters be born that day, the air rain blood,
The mother not recognise her own son.

May all the people, unwarned and confounded,
With tears upon their faces, colour fled,
Suppose destroyed the world already has been.

Fearful people, no need to be astounded,
For that day dropped upon the world a life
The most disparadised ever was seen.

Quando de minhas mágoas

Quando de minhas mágoas a comprida
Maginação os olhos me adormece,
Em sonhos aquella alma me apparece
Que para mim foi sonho nesta vida.

Lá n'huma soidade, onde estendida
A vista por o campo desfallece,
Corro apoz ella; e ella então parece
Que mais de mi se alonga, compellida.

Brado: Não me fujais, sombra benina!
Ela (os olhos em mi co'hum brando pejo,
Como quem diz, que ja não pode ser)

Torna a fugir-me: torno a bradar: *Dina...*
E antes que diga *mene,* acórdo, e vejo
Que nem hum breve engano posso ter.

To Dynamenë

When of my sufferings the long drawn out
'magination has brought sleep to my eyes,
to me in dream on dream there will arise
that soul who was, to me 'n this life, a dream.

There in a solitude where vision, strained
out over the plain, faints as it peers,
I run towards her; and she then appears
to move away from me, further, constrained.

I shout: Don't run from me, shade, so benign!
She (eyes on me in tender modesty,
like one who says that now it cannot be)

turns to escape me; and I, crying out: – *Dyne-*,
before I say *ámenë* wake, and see
that even a brief delusion's not for me.

Ah! minha Dinamene! assi deixaste

Ah! minha Dinamene! assi deixaste
Quem nunca deixar pôde de querer-te!
Que ja Nympha gentil, não possa ver-te!
Que tão veloz a vida desprezaste!

Como por tempo eterno te apartaste
De quem tão longe andava de perder-te?
Puderão essas ágoas defender-te
Que não visses quem tanto magoaste?

Nem somente fallar-te a dura morte
Me deixou, qu'apressada o negro manto
Lançar sôbre os teus olhos consentiste!

Oh mar! oh ceo! oh minha escura sorte!
Qual vida perderei que valha tanto,
Se inda tenho por pouco o viver triste?

Ah! My Dynamenë! So you have left

Ah! My Dynamenë! So you have left
one who will leave seeking for you?
Ah! My own nymph! I'll never see you now,
you have disdained this so wingèd thing, life.

Could you now separate yourself for ever
from one who's been so long without you? How?
Did these waves have the power to bar you
from ever seeing the man whom you so grieve?

Not ever to speak to you is left to me
by cruel death, so quickly you allowed
the black mantle over your eyes laid!

O sea, O Heaven, O my dusk destiny!
What pain have I to feel, that makes it so good
that I judge short the time still to live sad?

Verdade, Amor, Razão, Merecimento

Verdade, Amor, Razão, Merecimento,
Qualquer alma farão segura e forte;
Porém Fortuna, Caso, Tempo, e Sorte,
Tẽe do confuso mundo o regimento.

Effeitos mil revolve o pensamento,
E não sabe a que causa se reporte:
Mas sabe que o que he mais que vida e morte
Não se alcança de humano entendimento.

Doctos varões darão razões subidas;
Mas são as exp'riencias mais provadas:
E por tanto he melhor ter muito visto.

Cousas ha hi que passão sem ser cridas:
E cousas cridas ha sem ser passadas.
Mas o melhor de tudo he crer em Christo.

Truthfulness, Love, Reason and Excellence

Truthfulness, Love, Reason and Excellence
will make a soul in itself strong and carefree,
and yet Chance, Fortune, Time and Destiny
have of this turbid world the governance.

Thousand are the effects thought twists and turns
and does not see their cause, yet it does see
that what is more than life and death must be
beyond reach of human intelligence.

The learnèd give reasons grandly conceived
but trial and error is a test that's safer,
to have seen much is to be better advised.

Things there are, happen and are not believed,
and things believed there are that happened never,
but the all-best is to believe in Christ.

Hum mover de olhos, brando e piedoso

Hum mover de olhos, brando e piedoso
Sem ver de que; hum riso brando e honesto,
Quasi forçado; hum doce e humilde gesto,
De qualquer alegria duvidoso;

Hum despejo quieto e vergonhoso;
Hum repouso gravissimo e modesto;
Huma pura bondade, manifesto
Indicio da alma, limpo e gracioso;

Hum encolhido ousar; huma brandura;
Hum medo sem ter culpa; hum ar sereno;
Hum longo e obediente soffrimento:

Esta foi a celeste formosura
Da minha Circe, e o magico veneno
Que pôde transformar meu pensamento.

A movement of the eyes, kind, merciful

A movement of the eyes, kind, merciful,
not seeing on whom; a smile kindly and honest,
almost compelled; sweet and humble gestures
doubtful of any joy given or to feel;

an everyday behaviour shamefaced, still;
a repose very serious and modest;
a pure benevolence, the manifest
counterpart of the limpid, dainty soul;

a daring that was shy; a kindliness;
a serene air; fear with no guilty reason;
a long obedience there whenever sought;

these have been the celestial loveliness
of my own Circe, and the magic poison
which had the power to transform my thought.

I

Já se vião chegados junto á terra,
Que desejada já de tantos fôra,
Que entre as correntes Indicas se encerra,
E o Ganges, que no ceo terreno mora.
Ora, sus, gente forte, que na guerra
Quereis levar a palma vencedora,
Já sois chegados, já tendes diante
A terra de riquezas abundante.

II

A vós, ó geração de Luso, digo,
Que tão pequena parte sois no mundo;
Não digo inda no mundo, mas no amigo
Curral de quem governa o ceo rotundo:
Vós, a quem não somente algum perigo
Estorva conquistar o povo immundo,
Mas nem cobiça, ou pouca obediencia
Da Madre, que nos ceos está em essencia:

III

Vós, Portuguezes poucos, quanto fortes,
Que o fraco poder vosso não pesais;
Vós, que á custa de vossas várias mortes
A Lei da vida eterna dilatais:

Europe Rebuked
(The *Lusiads,* Canto 7, stanzas 1-10)

The Lusiads (Os Lusíadas, that is, the Portuguese) is the national epic of Portugal, called Lusitania by the Romans. The poem, published in 1572, celebrates Vasco da Gama's voyage to India in 1497–8: it consists of ten cantos running to 8,816 lines in *ottava rima,* the favourite epic form of the Italian Renaissance after Dante. At the beginning of the seventh canto the poet uses Vasco's arrival in India as an occasion to rebuke his fellow-Europeans for their lack of Christian solidarity.

I

And now they see that they are close to land
Which was the apple of so many eyes
With Indian streams lapping its every strand
And Ganges too, the earthly paradise.
Up now, strong people, whose unconquered band
Will lift the victor's palm into the skies:
Now you have come, now here before you stretches
The land that overflows with wealth and riches.

II

To you, O Lusitanians, I say
That to you such a small plot has been given
Not only in the world but equally
In his sweet fold who rules the curve of heaven –
You who not only are not turned away
By danger from subduing the unshriven
Nor yet by greed or disobedience
Of Mother Church, whose mansions are far hence.

III

So few and yet so strong, you Portuguese
Who by your puny numbers are not cowed
Who have afforded many deaths to blaze
One Law of everlasting life abroad.

Assi do ceo deitadas são as sortes,
Que vós, por muito poucos que sejais,
Muito façais na santa Christandade:
Que tanto, ó Christo, exaltas a humildade!

IV

Vede-los, Allemáes, soberbo gado,
Que por tão largos campos se apascenta,
Do successor de Pedro rebellado
Novo pastor, e nova seita inventa:
Vedo-lo em feas guerras occupado
(Que inda co'o cego errôr se não contrenta)
Não contra o superbissimo Othomano,
Mas por sahir do jugo soberano.

V

Vede-lo duro Inglez, que se nomea
Rei da velha e sanctissima Cidade,
Que o torpe Ismaelita senhorea,
(Quem vio honra tão longe da verdade!)
Entre as Boreaes neves se recrea,
Nova maneira faz de Christandade:
Para os de Christo tem a espada nua,
Não por tomar a terra, que era sua.

VI

Guarda-lhe por emtanto um falso Rei
A cidade Hierosolyma terrestre,
Emquanto elle não guarda a sancta lei
Da cidade Hierosolyma celeste.
Pois de ti, Gallo indigno, que direi?
Que o nome Christianissimo quizeste,
Não para defendê-lo, nem guarda-lo,
Mas para ser contra elle, e derriba-lo!

Thus heaven which decides our fate decrees
That you, although so few, have been endowed
To do great deeds as guardians of the holy:
How high, O Christ, do you lift up the lowly!

IV

Look at the Germans, those conceited cattle
Whose pasture is of such a huge extent
Who with the one in Peter's Chair did battle
And now new shepherd and new flock invent:
Look at them, busy with the sabre's rattle
Who in blind error still are not content
To take up arms against the heathen Turk
But labour to shake off the rightful yoke.

V

Look at the hard-faced Englishman, self-styled
King of the ancient city, that beloved
Shrine by the shameless son of Ishmael ruled
(Who from the truth saw honour so removed!):
Taking his ease among the northern cold
He fashions a new faith that none has proved
Baring his sword before the men of Christ
Not to recover land he once possessed.

VI

Meanwhile a false king holds against his might
Jerusalem, that city here below
While he spurns in the holy Law's despite
The high Jerusalem to which we go.
Now you, unworthy Frenchman, I indict:
You sought the name 'Most Christian' – wherefore? No
Not to defend it, give it your protection
But to attack it, bring about destruction.

VII

Achas, que tens direito em senhorios
De Christãos, sendo o teu tão largo e tanto,
E não contra o Cinypho e Nilo, rios
Inimigos do antiguo nome sancto?
Ali se hão de provar da espada os fios,
Em quem quer reprovar da Igreja o canto:
De Carlos, de Luiz, o nome e a terra
Herdaste, e as causas não da justa guerra?

VIII

Pois que direi daquelles, que em delicias,
Que o vil ocio no mundo traz comsigo,
Gastão as vidas, logrão as divicias,
Esquecidos de seu valor antigo?
Nascem da tyrannia inimicicias,
Que o povo forte tem de si inimigo:
Comtigo, Italia, fallo, já submersa
Em vicios mil, e de ti mesma adversa.

IX

O' miseros Christãos, pela ventura,
Sois os dentes de Cadmo desparzidos,
Que uns aos outros se dão a morte dura,
Sendo todos de um ventre produzidos?
Não vedes a divina sepultura
Possuida de cães, que sempre unidos
Vos vem tomar a vossa antigua terra,
Fazendo-se famosos pela guerra?

X

Vedes que tem por uso, e por decreto,
Do qual são tão inteiros observantes,
Ajuntarem o exercito inquieto
Contra os povos, que são de Christo amantes;

VII

Do you think that Christian lands are yours to claim
Although you have so many of your own
Careless to hear your holy ancient name
Spat on by Arab and barbarian?
Their lands are where the sword must find its fame –
On those who mock the Church's cornerstone:
From Charlemagne and Louis you have land
And name, which you lack courage to defend!

VIII

What shall I say of those who tread the ways
The world brings, and in idleness go rotten
Who in cheap pleasure wallow all their days
And all their ancient virtue have forgotten?
For a strong people breeds hostilities
And out of these tyranny is begotten:
You I call, Italy, sunk in a gulf
Of countless vices, turned against yourself.

IX

O miserable Christians! It would seem
That you are those same teeth which Cadmus sowed
Which though the offspring of a single womb
Tear at each other, strike each other dead:
Have you not noticed that the holy tomb
Is in the hands of Cain's united brood
Who come to you to take your ancient land
And reach for glory with a bloody hand?

X

You see them acting as their laws require
But gladly too, as to the manner born
Taking arms in a restless host to pour
On peoples who love Christ their fire and scorn:

Entre vós nunca deixa a fera Aleto
De semear cizanias repugnantes:
Olhai, se estais seguros de perigos,
Que elles e vós sois vossos inimigos.

Today the savage Furies never tire
Of sowing hateful tares among your corn.
Beware! From danger you are never free
When they and you are both your enemy.

translated by Keith Bosley

Appetite into Reason:
Love as experience in the lyric poetry of Camões

The principal themes in the lyric poetry of Camões are love and reason: love as a personal experience to be lived, rather than as an ideal to be served in the name of the Absolute Beauty propounded by the Renaissance neo-Platonists, and reason as the instrument for transforming experience into self-knowledge. Camões' concern with experience and knowledge makes him, perhaps, the first European poet who can properly be described as 'modern'. The Renaissance, backward-looking to the extent that it sought to reproduce and restore what was regarded as the higher order of the ancient world, destroyed the medieval order and created the need to find a new synthesis to replace it, since the restoration of the ancients had failed, after all, to provide one. The Aristotelian concept of 'natural law' gave way to the search for knowledge of what that law could be. The vision of the world as the result of a fall from a better state, whether the Garden of Eden, the world of Classical Antiquity or, in their mystical and poetic neo-Platonic sense, the Petrarchan 'stars' from which the divine in man had descended – was replaced by the awareness of the possibility that the fallen world could be improved. Utopias ceased to be allegories of God's creative intention to become models of possible worlds. Observation and experiment began to supersede scholastic deduction. The concept of man who, as microcosm of a presupposed universal order, was 'the measure of all things', acquired a new and daring dimension in the notion that the measure of man – microcosm of a universal order yet to be established – was his experience. Thus, the old structures of thought were filled in with new meanings. Camões, *nel mezzo del cammin* of his life in the mid-1550s, was to use the Petrarchan imagery still dominant in his time in the context of an understanding of the self and the world very different from, and at times the opposite of, that which such imagery had been created to depict and signify.

Almost all Camões' lyric poetry is love poetry. The same could be said, of course, of the poetry of Dante or Petrarch. But these poets, unlike Camões, did not see the *otherness* of the beloved woman as the cause of their impulse to love. Nor did they admit eroticism as the means of exploring that impulse. On the contrary, they saw the beloved as the amplifying ideal of themselves and eroticism as an obstacle to the attainment of that ideal. The biographical truth of their individual loves was submitted to the transmutation representative of a higher truth. Love becomes the means of ascent to an absolute. Camões transformed the beloved woman from symbol into reality and, as such, from the inevitable *one* (Beatrice, Laura) into the many, potentially and in fact.

In his sonnet 'Em quanto quis Fortuna que tivesse' (pp. 18-19) Camões warns the reader that the diverse loves in which love manifests itself in his verses are not faults or 'defects' – as they would have had to be regarded in strictly Petrarchan terms – but, *because* of their diversity, 'pure truths', which the reader himself, according to his own experience of love (thus subversively brought into the semantic area of the poem) can and should understand.

In many of his poems, there is a sexual urgency that delights in the demystification of the Petrarchan convention of courtly love still dominant in the European poetry of his time. This attitude is found in the two *redondilhas* (roundels) included in Jonathan Griffin's selection (pp. 20-23), with the mocking irreverence of their use of popular themes and metre. It can also be found in his more serious poems as, for example, in the third of his ten *canzoni*, a form Camões preferred to use for extended philosophical meditations. In this song, with its beautiful opening stanzas, the Petrarchan idealization of the lady to whom it is addressed is disrupted by the introduction of the theme of physical desire: the 'noble vision' of the beloved as an embodiment of the heavenly idea of Beauty is an ideal attainable only if desire does not intervene. But Camões is a 'man of flesh and bone' ('homem de carne e osso') and must live or die in the physical present. The song legitimizes the erotic impulse at the root of the ideal of beauty, using the prestige of the idealising model of love to ennoble eroticism, which is thus included in the model rather than abjured.

In dignifying the erotic, the love poetry of Camões marks a subtle and complex break with the past, at the same time reintegrating that past by using the imagery of the Petrarchan tradition to express the new modes of experience it seeks to explore and define. The sonnet 'Transforma-se o amador na cousa amada' (pp. 26-27) offers a striking illustration of this process. The concept of the transformation of the lover into beloved is central to the Renaissance neo-Platonists, Before Camões, it had already been used, in almost the same words, by Marsilio Ficino and by León Hebreo (Judah Abravanel) and, after Camões, by Saint John of the Cross to express his sensual mysticism ('amada en el Amado transformada!'). It is present, too, in Saint Teresa of Ávila's passionate injunction to God ('Devour me') and underlies Cathy's ardent statement in *Wuthering Heights:* 'I *am* Heathcliff – he's always, always in my mind … as my own being' Camões treats it, however, as a logical proposition and, as such, one to be debated, thus exposing it as a false metaphor. If the lover could indeed be transformed into the beloved 'by virtue of long imagining' and thus contain within himself the imagined beloved, the body should have no further cause for desire. And yet it continues to desire. Though the elimination or sublimation of desire is implicit in the spiritualising initial proposition, Camões, by qualifying its totalising truth, establishes desire as a reality whose value is equivalent, and complementary, to that of spiritual love, defining, in terms of the complementarity of the two types of love, his own love as both 'alive' and 'pure', a total response to the 'semi-divine' nature of the beloved (who, as demigoddess, is also half-human). Thus, the totality of love presupposes the act of love, which becomes the search of 'simple matter' for its 'form'.

Physical desire, which prevents any totalising idealisation of love, is also the spur to Camões' self-experiments conducted, libertinely (in the most noble sense of the word), through his exploration of love. In contraposition to the idealised man of the neo-Platonists, who could be integrated into a superhuman totality only in part – the physical dross thrown off in the spiritual pursuit – Camões proposed the ideal of his own human totality, the object of his search for self-knowledge. Love, with its inseparable erotic component, is for Camões a form of knowledge, rooted, like the profound truth learned by one who had 'experienced all and experimented with everything', in the dramatic awareness of the *other* and the consequent, and deeply moving, temporary unawareness of self which is central to love. Love thus becomes the means of exploring the unknown which Camões seeks to define and to become, in human and irreversible terms. In one of his sonnets he writes 'may blind love never tire in guiding me to that part from where I know not how to turn'. Knowing himself to have no knowledge – and all knowledge begins with its absence – Camões acknowledges his unknowing in the beautiful *canzone* 'Manda-me amor que cante docemente' (pp. 32-33). It is a state defined as the result of the interaction of the 'I', Nature, and the beloved, and the consequent reconciliation of all opposites, revealed to be, after all, complementary The need to connect, to make all life harmonious in the articulation of the different aspects of felt life, reveals the great 'concert' of the world whose cause, love, 'transforms appetite into reason'.

The transformation of appetite into reason is, in fact, the personal hypothesis on which Camões based his search for a synthesis which could reconcile the apparently contradictory elements in man. He tried to formulate this integrating synthesis in terms of his own destiny, using his experience as a bridge to the unknown and not, like the neo-Platonists of his time, to reinforce a presupposed idea of a hierarchical universal order.

Even in the most traditionally Petrarchan of his poems – and, as is only to be expected in a body of poetry which reflects the transition between two visions of the world, there are many such – there is almost always an element of novelty. This is the case of the famous elegiac sonnet imitated from Petrarch 'Alma minha gentil, que te partiste' (pp. 40-41) in which he registers the death of a beloved, generally identified as his slave and mistress Dynamenë (addressed by name in other poems), whose dark beauty was in such striking contrast to that of the Ideal Beauty personified in Petrarch's fair Laura. Apostrophising her as his 'gentle soul', it is in terms of the 'burning' and 'pure' love she witnessed in his eyes – which he begs her not to forget in that 'ethereal seat' to which she has now risen – that he longs to be reunited with her. This vision of Paradise, foreseeing the continuation, on another plane, of the love experienced on earth and not the spiritual transmutation that would exclude the sensual *and* pure delight of 'seeing', is neither Petrarchan nor Christian. The glorification of a love which is of this world is, however, not surprising in the work of a poet whose vision of the earthly Paradise in *The Lusiads* is one of eroticism triumphant: the reward which Venus gives the returning Portuguese heroes, who copulate ecstatically with the goddess Tethys (daughter of Uranus and Vesta) and her sea-nymphs, is a paradise of the senses. But Tethys has also come to the mariners 'at the bidding of immutable destiny' to unfold to them, through the gift of prophecy, the 'remaining secrets of the sphere'. The erotic thus brings with it a vision of the universal harmony in the 'mighty fabric of creation, ethereal and elemental'. It is interesting to note that the epic episode of the 'joyous lovers' isle' uses, like the Dynamenë sonnet, one of Petrarch's poems as specific reference. But Petrarch's 'Triumph of Love' is conceived as the absence of desire, the very opposite of the unregenerate sexuality of the island of love.

In another context, Camões explicitly criticizes the contemporary falsities of Petrarchan love in the words of Duriano, the amusing 'rake' who is one of the characters in his play *Filodemo*. The tone is the good-humoured irreverence that characterizes the innumerable *redondilhas* in which Camões seems to be using his poetic talents merely to persuade reluctant mistresses to share the sexual delights he so enticingly advertises: 'all you others, who love in the passive, claim that love as fine as a melon must desire no more of its mistress than to love her; and along comes your Petrarch and your Peter Bembo, towed by three hundred Platos, more threadbare than the gloves of my page, artfully stating the verisimilar and apparent reasons why you should seek no more of your mistress than to have her in your sight; and at the very most to speak with her. And you will find yet others, minute observers of love, who are more speculative and who will engage in knightly jousts, if need be, not to impregnate desire; but I shall swear most solemnly that if any of these lovers were to be presented with his mistress, neatly trussed and caparisoned between two plates, no stone would be left standing on stone. And for myself I must confess that my loves shall be in the active: she shall be the patient and I the agent. For this, I say, is the truth.'

Camões is not, of course, simply another Duriano, whose earthy sensuality leaves no room for questioning eroticism itself. This Camões does in the extraordinary sonnet 'Em prisões baixas fui hum tempo atado' (pp. 54-55). In this sonnet, the metaphorical prisons of 'base' sensuality are, in a further articulation of love and life, juxtaposed with the real gaols whose chains he had also experienced. He recognizes that the unknown which he had sought to explore and to become, by making himself its probe, is finally unknowable: 'blind Death and dubious chance'. Tragically, he begins to understand the nature of his destiny, his 'star': he has learned to fear joy.

The 'unreason of the world' becomes an obsessive theme. Nature is seen to be alien to human suffering· it remains aloof in its beautiful, ample, and neutral calm while man mourns his lost love. This insight finds poignant expression in the sonnet 'O ceo, a terra, o vento socegado' (pp. 38-39) in which the anguished voice of the fisherman Aónio is carried away by the wind in the 'restful silence of the night'. Like Nature, God is neutral and remains outside the dramas of the human soul and its world. It is a world in which 'Truth, Love, Reason, Moral Worth' are opposed to 'Fortune, Chance, Time and Fate', the former making the soul 'secure and strong', the latter having rule of the 'confused world'. The sonnet which opens with these stated antinomies progresses in a series of antithetical parallels, whose reconciliation is sought in vain since there is no possibility of discovering any plan in the world's unreason. Faith seems to be no more than the recognition of the final failure of human thinking, the impossibility of reconciling these antinomies. It is simply that which intervenes once thought has recognized that 'human understanding cannot grasp what is beyond life and death'. Christ, alien and neutral, who enters the scheme abruptly in the last line of the sonnet, personifies the human impossibility of understanding what lies beyond life and death, but does not seem to offer an alternative, regenerative understanding of the labyrinthine universe that lies within life and death. He seems to be its negation and its opposite: the total absence which, from the viewpoint of the apparent world postulated by the poem, is the antithetical equivalent of the Plotinian concept of evil as the absolute absence of good.

In this view, the concepts of God and Nature, seen as neutral in relation to individual human destinies, are disturbingly close to the concept of Death, whose presence becomes increasingly felt in the structure of Camões' lyric poetry. In the sonnet 'Cá nesta Babilonia' (pp. 58-59), the biblical-Platonic metaphor of a Zion which is the antithesis of Babylon can be understood in an orthodox way. Zion is at once a metaphysical state of lost perfection and a personal state of lost happiness opposed to the chaos of the confused labyrinth which is the world of the present. But in a complementary sonnet which uses the same imagery, 'Na ribeira do Euphrates assentado' (pp. 56-57), the traditional contrast between Zion and exile (both physical and metaphysical) is chillingly associated with a longing for death. Yearning for the lost glory of Zion has become too great to bear and the songs of Zion can no longer be sung: the only 'pious remedy' is 'to sing of nothing but death'.

The world seems to be 'no more than God's forgetfulness' and life 'no more than what it seems' This terrible, almost heretical, suggestion of the non-immanence of the transcendent God in his creation is made in the sonnet 'Correm turbas as águas deste rio' (pp. 52-53). Here the recurrent theme of the world's unreason and the conclusion that life is meaningless – which seems to be the bitter knowledge gained by Camões in his probing of the unknown – finds possibly its highest expression.

At the complementary level of the individual human condition, Camões, who has used his own destiny as the means of exploring the nature of the unknown, links his personal situation to that of the world in the sonnet which opens with the question 'What can I now ask the world?' (pp. 42-43). His attempt to live out life's contradictions – which, for the world to have made sense, would have had to prove complementary in the synthesis he could finally have defined from the experience thus lived – has led him to recognize that he was, after all, no more than a passive object. Life has lived him. Having 'seen all', knowing that even death does not come when it should, since 'great grief does not kill', he knows too that he can now 'look on anything'. From his apprenticeship, the experience he so valued, he has learned that he has 'now lost that which the loss of fear' had 'taught' him. The tragic nihilism which makes the world appear no more than God's oversight, and life in the world no more than what it seems, is rooted in Camões' own tragedy: to have been born only to experience the 'dislove' in the world and the 'great grief of death'.

In the sonnet 'Erros meus, má fortuna, amor ardente' (pp. 48-49), the errors, evil fortune and fervent love which have characterised his life are conjured up to accuse and damn him. Yet love alone would have sufficed him, even though he has seen only its 'brief lures'. But having 'lived all', he has learned 'never more to want to be content' and has recognized that he has 'blotted all the discourse' of his 'years'. In this remarkable line the writing in which he recorded the project of himself – the 'discourse' which was not only the course of his life but also reason, the act of understanding by which he passed from its premises to its consequences, and its narration – is fused with the project itself.

The 'discourse' of his life, now seen to be an 'error' and not the human totality he had sought to achieve through the search for self-knowledge through experience, has revealed only the terrible labyrinth of errors which the world has proved to be. Thus, the sonnet 'O dia em que nasci' (pp. 60-61) is a black malediction on the day of his birth, seen as a horrible portent of the end of the world. In this inversion of values, individual destiny is so bound up with the destiny of the world that a universal holocaust must accompany the death of a day which 'dropped upon the world' a life which has come to be seen as no more than yet another unreason in the world's unreason.

The consequences of the failure of Camões' life-long project to transmute appetite into reason through the experience of love, using reason to gain knowledge, are taken further in the long poem 'Super Flumina': Camões finds Christ. The poem, a gloss on Psalm 137, 'By the rivers of Babylon', uses the imagery of Babylon and Zion to develop the theme of Mutabilitie. The impermanent and fleeting world, ruled by mutability with its accidents, temporal rubs and hindrances, is the world of exile where the poet hangs his harp upon the willows, as trophy to his vanquisher Babylon, the alien land, is the land of flesh ('Babylon's daughter') which has 'bruised the soul', and must consequently 'with cruel discipline' be bruised in turn. Zion is the true fatherland, the land to which Camões says he will return, a *penitent,* to rest eternally. Christ is the Captain of Zion, whose divine Flesh on the Cross will save the soul from the 'vices of the evil flesh'.

This vision of an orthodox redeeming Christ is sharply contrasted with the vision of the alien Christ, beyond human understanding, of the sonnet on the antinomies ('Truthfulness, Love, Reason, Excellence'). Before this primitive Christ, Camões unmakes the former project of himself, renounces his earthly songs, repudiates all he has tried to be, know and reveal. The final triumph of the Counter-Reformation and the beginning of the long night through which Portugal was to live, crystallised in the individual destiny of its greatest poet? The parallel is tempting and the temptation is not original. Camões, old, suffering from the physical and spiritual diseases love had brought him, tired, poor and disillusioned, had ceased to search for a new humanist synthesis in which the traditional culture from which he had emerged could be reconciled with the new man he had already become. Instead, he plunged into a ferociously orthodox Catholicism and, immersed in its dogma, offered his contrite flesh to a Christ who represents the final triumph of death as the end and reason of life. Yet not even in these last years did eroticism become a marginal or philosophically irrelevant element in the structure of his poetry: The mortification of the flesh which becomes the spur to salvation in the gloss on Psalm 137 is still a recognition, negative and perverse though it is, of his condition as 'a man of flesh and bone'. His search for a humanist synthesis may have failed but Camões could never ignore the flesh – he had to destroy it.

HÉLDER MACEDO
London, February 1976

Biographical Information

Luís Vaz de Camões (?1524–1580) is Portugal's national poet, and the author of the national epic, *Os Lusíadas* (The Lusiads), which also appears in the Shearsman Classics series in the earliest English translation (1655), by Sir Richard Fanshawe.

Jonathan Griffin (1906–1990) was educated at Radley College and New College, Oxford. He wrote topical books on military matters in the 1930s. During World War Two he was Director of BBC European Intelligence and was ultimately responsible for the Victory sign, made famous by Winston Churchill. For the first few years after the war, Griffin was responsible for cultural and educational matters at the British Embassy in Paris.

He resigned from the Foreign Office in 1951 and thereafter devoted himself to writing poetry and plays, subsidising his literary activities by translating prose books from the French. These translations included the first volume of General de Gaulle's memoirs, the memoirs of Jean-Louis Barrault, the plays of Henri de Montherlant, novels by Jean Giono and Romain Gary, art criticism by Dora Vallier and René Huyghe, and the cinematographic notebooks of Robert Bresson.

Griffin's long and complex verse play, *The Hidden King*, was performed at the Edinburgh Festival in 1957. Despite poor reviews it was a popular success but, like other practitioners of poetic drama, he went out of fashion with the onset of 'kitchen sink' theatre. Between 1957 and 1983, he published seven books of poetry. He lived long enough to see his *Collected Poems* published in the U.S.A. in two volumes (1989 and 1990). The poet and critic Jonathan Delamont made a selection of Griffin's best poems for the Menard Press, London, and these were published as *In Earthlight* in 1995.

Admired as a poet by Ted Hughes and others, Jonathan Griffin is probably best known as a distinguished translator of poetry and plays, mainly from the French, Portuguese and German. The plays include Kleist's *The Prince of Homburg* and Claudel's *Break of Noon*. His main poetry translations were of Fernando Pessoa (several volumes including the Penguin Modern European Poets edition of Pessoa), Camões and René Char.

Hélder Macedo (1935–) was born in South Africa and raised in Mozambique; he spent his adolescence in Portugal, with extended stays in Guinea-Bissau and São Tome e Principe. He studied Law at the University of Lisbon, and read Literature and History at King's College, London, where he obtained a Ph.D and was later the Camões Professor of Portuguese for twenty-two years. He has published many collections of poems, several novels, and a number of volumes of criticism, including works on Camões.

JORGE DE SENA (1919–1978) was a Portuguese poet, critic, essayist, novelist, dramatist, translator and university professor. He lived in Brazil (1959–65) and spent his remaining years in the United States, teaching at the University of California at Santa Barbara.

He was the author of the standard history of English literature in Portuguese, and the translator into that language of hundreds of poems from several literatures, ancient and modern, collected now in four volumes. His studies on Camões (begun with a lecture in 1948, which was somewhat of a scandal) – collected in three volumes and also scattered in learned publications in several languages (the major article on Camões in the *Encyclopaedia Britannica* is his) – placed him in the forefront of Camões criticism, and forced a revision of all the traditional approaches to the poet and his works. His view of Camões as an almost heretical mind, with many Jewish undertones, and a very critical patriot have challenged those traditions, and his structural and textural studies have reopened the case for a definitive edition of Camões' works.

www.ingramcontent.com/pod-product-compliance
Lightning Source LLC
Chambersburg PA
CBHW022202080426
42734CB00006B/551